'DENIM' FINISHES

by

RISHAB MANOCHA

ACKNOWLEDGEMENT

My sincere gratitude to everyone in VF Arvind Brands Pvt. Ltd. for giving me the opportunity to work with them and successfully complete this Paper.

INTRODUCTION TO VF CORPORATION

VF is more than the world's largest apparel company. They're a dynamic, global powerhouse with more than $7.7 billion in annual revenues, over 30 dynamic lifestyle brands and over 47,000 associates working in locations across the globe.

Their brands are sold in more than 150 countries through 47,000 retailers in all channels of distribution, from mass to department to specialty retailers. In addition, they own and operate more than 780 retail stores. Many of their brands also sell products directly to consumers over the Internet. The leading VF owned bands are

Sourcing and manufacturing are managed through their Global Supply Chain organization, which oversees the production of 500 million items annually at more than 1,400 owned or sourced facilities in locations around the world.

Their business is organized across four key global regions.

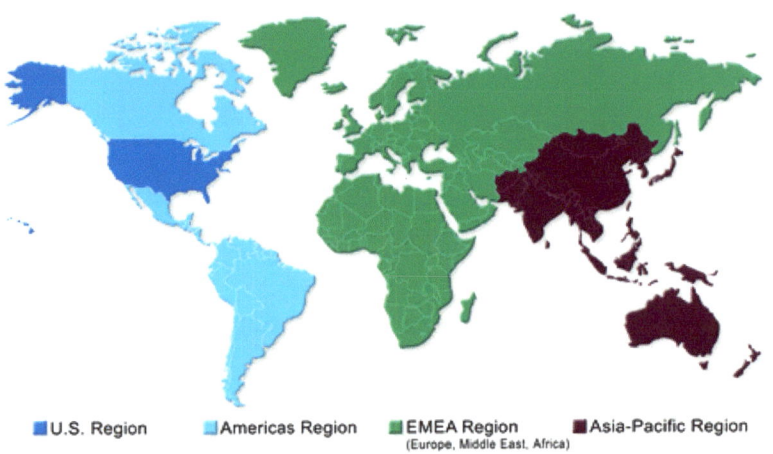

■U.S. Region ■Americas Region ■EMEA Region ■Asia-Pacific Region
(Europe, Middle East, Africa)

Asia-Pacific Region

The Asia-Pacific region plays an important role for both consumer product sales and VF's global sourcing operation. VF's brands are sold to retailers both directly and through licensees and distributors. In addition, VF's global sourcing operation is based in Hong Kong.

In India, VF markets Wrangler, Lee, Nautica, JanSport and Kipling products through VF Arvind Brands Private Ltd., a majority-owned joint venture located in Bangalore.

India

In 2006, a joint venture, VF Arvind Brands Private Ltd., is established with Arvind Mills Ltd., the third largesg denim manufacturer in the world, and the largest denim manufacturers in Asia, to design market and distribute VF branded products in India. The joint venture, VF Arvind Brands Private Ltd., initially encompassed VF's Lee, Wrangler, Nautica, JanSport and Kipling brands, which were previously marketed under licensing and distribution agreements with Arvind Fashions Ltd., a subsidiary of Arvind Mills Ltd., and serves as the vehicle for launching additional brands in India in the future. VF owns 60% of the joint venture, and Arvind Mills, Ltd. owns 40%

HISTORY OF LEE

The Lee Company was found in the year 1889 in Kansas, USA by H.D. Lee. Initially called the HD Lee Mercantile company it was a wholesale grocery company. In 1910, the company started manufacture of work wear from its plant. In 1913, Lee produced the Union-All which is a union of a jacket and a dungaree, the first in series of innovations which has characterized the company's long history. In 1943 the company was re-christened The HD Lee Company reflecting the growing importance of apparel in the company's fortunes. In 1969, The HD Lee Company was acquired by VF Corporation. The brand has since then been the property of VFC. Today Lee is one of the best known jeans wear and casual clothing brands in the world. Lee is present over 150 countries in the world.

The HD Lee Company has always led in innovation and style. The following are some of the path breaking innovations of the HD Lee Company which has helped shape the jeans wear industry over the years.

- 1913 - Produced the Lee Union-All
- 1925 - Launched the lightweight Jelt Denim with twisted yarn and unsurpassed durability
- 1926 - Launched the world's first zipper fly jeans – 101Z
- 1943 - Created the lazy S icon, which is a standard feature on all the Lee jeans now.
- 1952 - Launched the Chetopa Twill, a tough sharp looking work wear fabric.
- 1954 - Launched Leesures to cater to the leisure sportswear market.
- 1964 - Launched the no-iron permanent press slacks sold under the 'Lee- prest' name.
- 1979 - Launched the youth wear division achieving HD Lee's ambition of "Lee fits America"
- 1982 - Started using pumice stone for wash.
- 2002 - Launched the Lee Performance Khakis with nano care technology, creating a completely stain resistant yet breathable garment.

LEE IN INDIA

Lee was launched in India in the year 1995. The brand was launched under a license agreement with VF Corporation, by Arvind Fashion Limited. Which is 2006 is turned into a joint venture; VF Arvind Brands Private Ltd. Lee was launched in the country with the tag line "The Jeans that built America". The campaign successfully helped in establishing the heritage and the American connection to the brand. The execution of the advertisement, which showed a group of people clothing the famous twin tower with a pair of Lee jeans, established the functionality of the product I.e., innovative and durable.

At the time of launch Lee also built a strong association with music, especially rock music. As part of the brand campaign Lee sponsored the 'A to Z of Rock' on Channel V, the leading music channel at that time. Internationally too Lee has had a strong association with rock music with Bruce Springsteen being one of the famous brand ambassadors.

 Leesures by Lee, the sub-brand for non-denim garments was added in the year 1997. The range was launched with one of the first wrinkle free trousers to be made in the country. The campaign reflected action & outdoor and was not focused on a 'corporate setting' which one was used to in a trouser advertisement.

There were many firsts associated with the launch of lee in India. Lee was the first band of jeans wear to:-

- Open exclusive stores/ outlets
- Offer a wide range in fits, fabrics and styles, for guys and girls and offer multiple inseam length.
- Launch with a national television campaign
- have a WAP site, giving customers virtually everything
- introduce an exclusive in-store radio called Radio 18.89-The Sound of Denim, a radio station that plays same music same time across all Lee stores.

LEE CONSUMER PROFILE

- Young, 16-28 years of age
- Urban
- Male or female
- Exposed to current 'global' fashion trends and willing to adopt these trends
- Socially active, popular within peer group and sophisticated
- Willing to pay a premium for quality

LEE BRAND POSITIONING

- Young
- Cool
- Fashionable
- Charismatic
- Urban & American
- With long heritage but always relevant and never 'out of fashion'

PROCESS WORKFLOW OF THE COMPANY

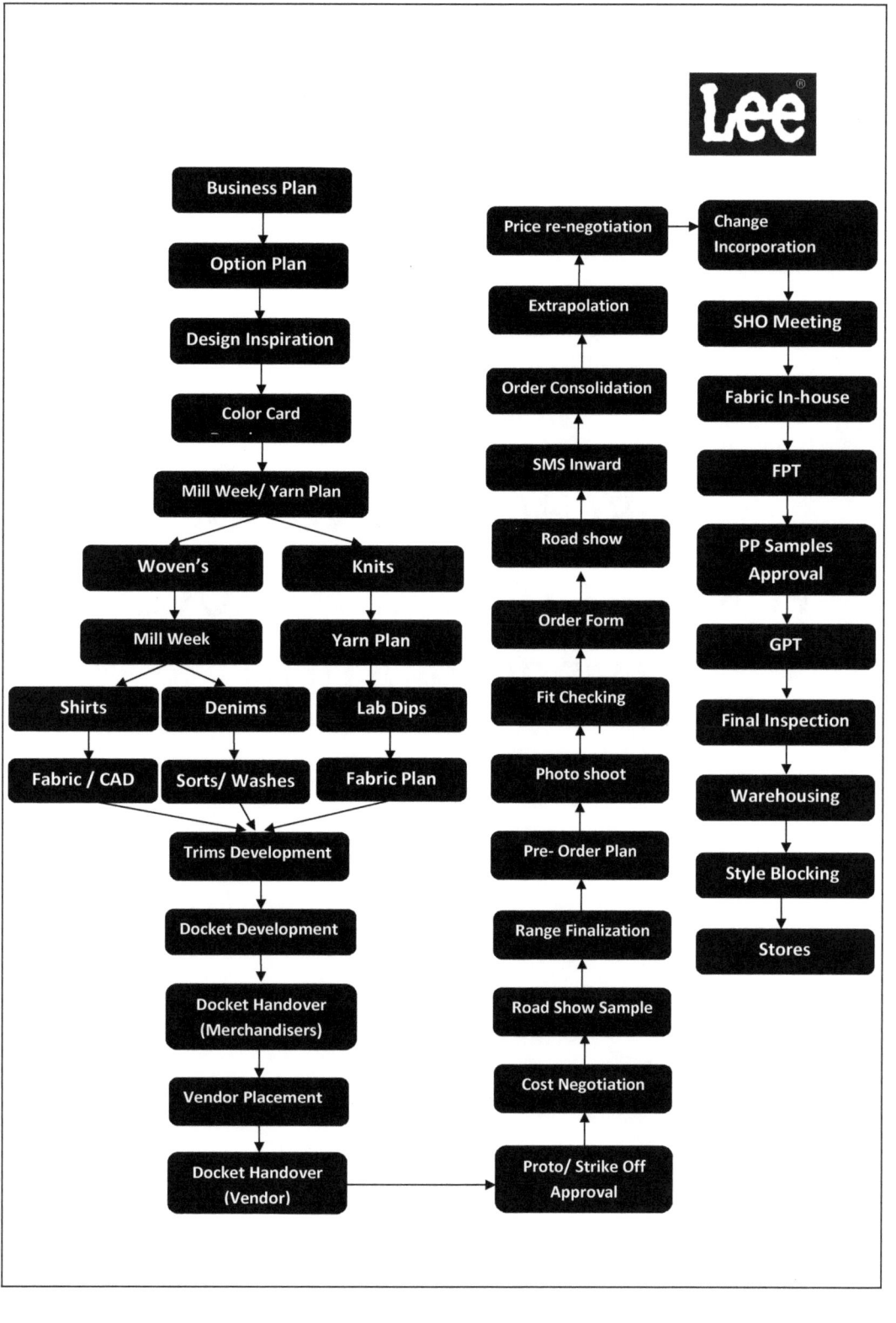

MERCHANDISING SOP

FORMULATION AND PROCESS

IMPROVISATION

MERCHANDISING

Merchandiser-A Data Bus between Buyer & Seller

Merchandiser is he who builds up relationship with the buyer and acts as a seller. He plays a vital role in an organization in a sense that he bears more responsibility than other in regards to execution of an order. The responsibilities that he bears on the jobs are as follows:

He represents as a buyer to the factory.

He represents as a seller to the buyers.

He inspects Quality as a buyer (from the buyer's point of view).

He looks into the business to flourish more in future.

He tries to add value to the brand, by bringing forward creative inputs.

He tries to offer the deal more competitive without compromising the Quality.

His object is to satisfy the buyers to progress more of the future business.

His aim is to impress the buyers by means of

- Right Product
- Right Quality
- Right Quantities
- Schedule Time

AIM

The aim of my project is to study the functioning of Lee, knits department, try finding the loopholes in the procedure that causes miscommunication with the vendors, which leads to unsatisfactory outcomes and delays. Once found, I would make a standard operational procedure, which would help to produce better outputs within the given lead-time.

RESEARCH METHODOLOGY

1. Study the functioning of Lee Knits department.
2. Evaluate the loopholes that cause miscommunication with the vendors and delays in sampling.
3. Device methods to minimize the problems faced
4. Make a Standard Operational Procedure for Lee, knits department, for a better and smoother workflow

PROBLEM AREAS

SAMPLE STAGE

1. Variation in fabric color in the same pantone shade form vendor to vendor
2. Miss-match between the fabric line plan and docket placement.
3. Delay in artwork submission
4. Unsatisfactory outcomes in the final road show samples even after strike off approval.
5. Miscommunication with the vendor with trims
6. Unorganized format of sample delivery
7. Use of stock fabric for yarn dyed stripers.
8. Open Costing given in different formats.
9. SMS inward to warehouse.

PRODUCTION STAGE

1. Record of FPT and GPT approvals

QUALITY MATTERS

1. Difference in cuff and body color after a few washes
2. Garment wash elimination

SAMPLE STAGE

1. Variation in fabric color in the same pantone shade form vendor to vendor

Problem

When the color story and the fabric order plan is made. The vendors send out their fabrics for dying. In many cases there is a variation in the same color from vendor to vendor, and then finally we have to either re-dye the fabric or use stock fabric, which leads to unfavorable circumstances.

Suggestion

Ideally, if we could assign one pantone shade to just one vendor and have them do the style of that comes into that color range, doing so will remove the problem of difference in shade vendor to vendor. But since this practically cannot be done, the alternate could be the following.

We should make it mandatory that, before the fabrics are sent for dying, the vendors must send us a lab dip for approval. If it is not approved, then they should not be allowed to proceed. Also, to help things better, we could provide the vendors with the ΔE value of our pantone colors, as this would make the color difference negligible. Also, I have made a little addition to our already existing fabric line plan that we provide to our vendors. They will have to jus fill in if the lab dip was approved and if so which one.

2. **Miss- match between fabric line plan and docket placement**

Problem

Once the color story has been decided, the designers make a fabric order plan, in which they assign the number of options that will be assigned to each color, in each delivery, and fabric. In accordance to this, they place the fabric order to the respective vendors, so that it can be dyed in advance and kept ready for sampling.

But, when the designers place their design dockets, they sometimes, lose track of this fabric order plan, which leads to an imbalance between numbers of options assigned to a particular color. This, in turn leads to shortage in certain color fabrics. The vendor then, has to re-send fabrics for dying and thus this leads to delay in sample development. Also, certain color which aren't used to its actual plan, ends up being unnecessarily added to the number of option in each style (jus for the purpose of exhausting the fabric) which sometimes reaches to 4 options in many styles, which would anyway be dropped in the final short-listing of options (as mostly only 2 options are selected in each style).

Suggestion

I have found a simple formulae, which if we apply to our excel master grids, it would highlight the cells, in which the same color in the same fabric is occurring more than twice. So, at this very stage we could ask the designers to re-assigns colors to certain styles, so that there is a balance among all colors and things go according to the fabric line plan.

=SUMPRODUCT (($B$2:$B$13=$B2)*($C$2:$C$13=$C2))>2

THE REVISED LINE PLAN FOR VENDORS

Vendor	ESSTEE
Tees	Line Plan - SS-12
GSM	170-180
Count / gg	30's/28gg
Fabric Finish	Bio-wash
Trims	Heavy Twill/ Canvas
	1/2" Height Velvet tape
	1/2" Height Compact Twill Tape
	1x1 lycra rib

Del 1	Color Name	Pantone #	Fabric qty in kg	Lab Dip Submission Date	Lab Dip Approval				Fabric In House Date
					A	B	C	D	
Col 1	Crown Jewel	P19-3640	10	10th Oct	██				10th Nov
Col 2	Pansy	P19-3542	10	10th Oct					
Col 3	Factory Blue	P18-4530	10	10th Oct		██			
Col4	Sunset Red	P19-2047	10	10th Oct			██		
Col 5	Total Eclipse	P19-4010	10	10th Oct		██			
Col 6	Red Jasper	P18-1643	10	10th Oct					
Col 7	Stormy grey	P18-0201	10	10th Oct					
Col 8	Rider Grey	P17-5102	10	10th Oct	██				
Col 9	Zest	P15-0548	10	10th Oct	██				
Col 10	Teal	P18-4535	10	10th Oct					
Col 11	Black		10	10th Oct	██				
Col 12	White		10	10th Oct	██				
Del 3									
Col 1	Moonlight Blue	P18-4027	10	10th Oct			██		
Col 2	Menthol	P16-5919	10	10th Oct			██		
Col 3	Coral	P17-1644	10	10th Oct			██		
Col 4	Golden Orange	P16-1346	10	10th Oct	██				
Col 5	Splash	P14-4811	10	10th Oct	██				
Col 6	Turquoise	P16-4834	10	10th Oct	██				
Col 7	Shady Green	P18-5624	10	10th Oct	██				
Col 8	Black		10	10th Oct	██				
Col 9	White		10	10th Oct				██	
Col 10	Grey Mélange		10	10th Oct		██			

3. **Delay in artwork submission**

Problem

Sometimes the dockets are placed on time, but the artworks are delayed for very long. The vendors receiving the dockets without the artwork can't begin with their work as most of the t-shirts are basic Bryan or rock fit. So there isn't much need for the proto samples.

Suggestion

I suggest that we should make it a point to turn in the artworks within one week from the the docket placement to the vendors. This way, they can begin with the screen development and printing immediately.

4. **Unsatisfactory outcomes in the final road show samples even after strike off approval.**

Problem

Once the fit sample is approved and they start sending strike-offs for approval, they then proceed to making the road-show samples in the different color ways. Once we receive them, we do not like the outcome of the color or size of embroidery/print in the different color ways, hence, we ask the vendors to re-do certain samples with the corrections made, this in-turn leads to delay, as the vendor has to re-make a sample and go through the whole process again.

Suggestion

Once the strike offs have been approved, we should ask the vendor to send a sample in its actual form, i.e., using the actual fabric with the appliqué or print and trims, within 10 days after the strike off approvals. Along with that they should send us the strike offs of the prints in all the color ways so that the designers can go through it at this very stage and ask them to make the required changes. This would save us a lot more time, and make it easier for both the vendor and us.

5. **Miscommunication with the vendor with trims**

Problem

When we release the dockets, we mention certain specific details, but not the basic details. The vendors assume the basic details on their own and make the changes, which are not pleasant and change the look of the garment as a whole, which again leads to reworking on the style and hence causes delay in delivery.

Suggestion

We need to make a standard trims layout, which all the vendors must follow, unless specifically mentioned in the dockets. I have made a reference grid, which could be followed

6. **Unorganized format of sample delivery**

   Problem

   We don't have a lot of small deadlines that we give to the vendor, because of which the vendors are not very up- to- date with their approval dispatches. This leads to delays in approval for certain styles, and thus delay the final road show sample, or, last minute deliveries which cause a lot of hassles on our end.

   Suggestion

   We need to have a layout, in which dates for the various approvals are given; also it should have the basic details on their courier, which they need to fill in while dispatching their samples.

7. **Use of stock fabric for yarn dyed stripers**

   Problem

   We have seen over the past seasons that the sell-through of our yarn dyed stripers has been very high. Yet we use the stock fabric that is available. This leads to the yarn dyed stripers stand out from the rest of our collection, which somewhere is not right.

   Suggestion

   I suggest that we develop the CADs for the yarn dyed stripers, keeping in mind our color cards and theme. This would make the yarn dyed stripers more synchronized with the rest of the collection. The CAD inputs should be given to the vendors 2 months prior to the docket placement, just like we do for shirts.

8. **Open Costing given in different formats**

   Problem

   Some of the vendors do not provide us with their open costing, also the once that do, put in their own format, which is difficult to analyze by us, as all the components are not included clearly. This makes it difficult for us to figure out where the vendors are keeping their buffer costs.

   Suggestion

   When we give the dockets to the vendors, we should give them the format of our open costing sheets and make it mandatory for them to fill it in and send it back when the road show samples start coming in. With the help of the open costing, we would come to know where the vendors are keeping the buffer profits. Through this we would know the tentative cost of the garments.

This should be done because a lot of styles get dropped during the range finalization because the quoted prices by the vendors are too high and we don't achieve the markup profit.

9. SMS inward to warehouse

Problem

Once the main roadshow is over we move on to the regional roadshows. For this the SMS are first sent by the vendors to the warehouse, where they pack the samples in different in different cartons according to the regions that they have to be sent to for the roadshow. The samples tend to get miss-placed in this whole process. Also, it takes more time for the samples to reach the venue as the samples go through this process and as the product team is travelling at this point of time it gets difficult for them to follow-up at each stage.

Suggestion

I suggest that at the time of PO creation itself we change the destination of the garments to be sent to directly their respective regions. The vendors would have to complete all the samples and pack them in different cartons for the four regions and directly forward it there. This way it will be comparatively easier for the product team to know the status of things. Also there will be lesser hassle during the SMS sending; also we would save time by not including the warehouse exercise.

PRODUCTION STAGE

1. Record of FPT and GPT approvals

We usually don't keep a record of the FPT and GPT during our production stage. Keeping a record of this will help us look into which vendors usually fail in which parameters of these tests and will allow us to allocate our styles better. I have made a simple chart which we can fill when the test reports come in.

QUALITY MATTERS

1. Difference in cuff and collar and body color after a few washes

We always here of complains about the knit polo styles that, after a few washes there seems to be a considerate difference in the color of the body and the cuff and collar of the polo.

If we use a compact 4 ply yarn with four course of lycra, for the collar and cuff of the polo's the color retained will be higher, and the polo's will not have the differentiation in color so soon. Also, we must make it mandatory for the vendors to use the rib collar and cuff to be 40gms

heavier than the body fabric. This will make the collar stand sharp and give a better visual appeal to the garments.

2. Garment wash elimination

During the sample development, we assign various washes to the garment, namely, fabric bio wash, panel wash, garment wash, etc. and we always do a garment bio wash. When we finally sit for the range and price finalization of the garments, we usually tend to outdo with the garment bio wash, to reduce our cost, and ask the vendors to remake the garments without it. This again takes extra time, and causes delays in the delivery of our road show samples, as the range finalization happens right in the end.

I suggest that initially we don't go garment bio-wash to any of our styles and let the samples come in. After seeing the outcome, we could ask our vendors to do a garment bio wash in the required styles and re-send the samples just for the wash. This will reduce the time consumption in re-making the garment and also provide us with out desired outcomes.

3. Hand feel references to be developed

We should develop a directory of standards of washes that matches our requirements. We could give it to our vendors for reference when they develop the washes, this would make it clear to them of the required level of hand feel that they need to maintain.

COMPARATIVE STUDY BETWEEN TWO LAUNDRIES BASED ON VISUAL AND COSTING ASPECT

AND

COMPETITIVE FIT MAPPING FOR WOMENS FITS WITH NEW DEVELOPMENTS

PROJECT BRIEF

INTRODUCTION

Denim is clearly a global presence, it not only exists in every country in the world, but in many of these it has become the single most common form of everyday attire.

The ultimate display of detail is found in true vintage denim. The story of each wearer has been indelibly recorded on each pair- each abrasion pattern, area of wear and whiskering, each grease stain are tell tale signs of what each pair has lived through. To achieve this effect naturally takes years of wearing in dry denim without washing- the patinas created through wear are completely personal to you and tell a very special story.

This also takes a great deal of patience. A lot of blood sweat and tears has gone into discovering techniques to speed up denim aging and wear processes that produce a naturally vintage look. The majority of this very skilled work is done by hand and the process is very time consuming.

My aim is to decode every step that takes place in achieving this look.

AIM

The aim of my project is to study the process that goes down behind denim washes, the cost that is incurred at every step. Once found, I will do a comparative study between two washing laundries of Lee. This comparative study will help the team to allocate their designs to the laundries efficiently, as I will provide them with information of which laundry is producing better results in which processes – visually. Also, I will do a comparative study on the cost breakdown of both the laundries, and find out the reason for the difference in their pricing and suggest for which process , which laundry is offering better price for competitive pricing of garment which will lead to cost saving and hence more profitability.

Source - http://www.oki-ni.com/page/denimfinishesandwashes

Denim Fabric Manufacturing Process

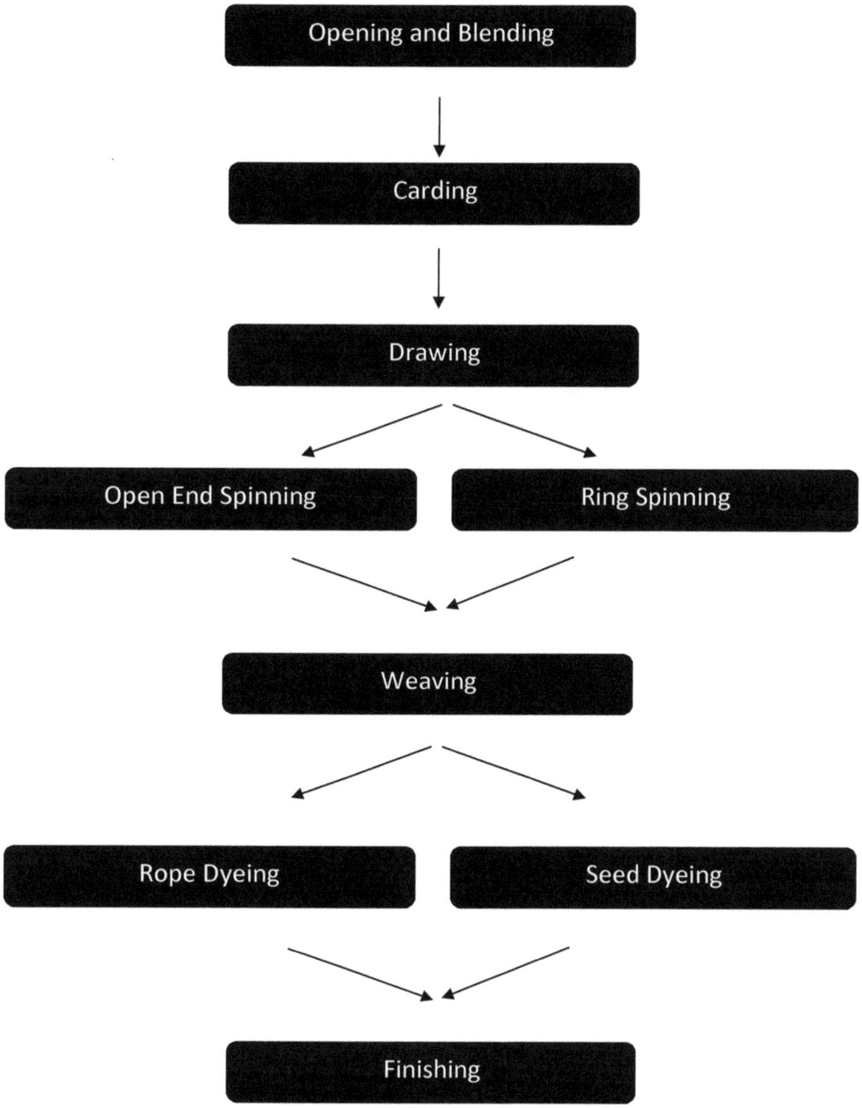

```
            ┌─────────────────────────┐
            │  Opening and Blending   │
            └─────────────────────────┘
                         │
                         ▼
            ┌─────────────────────────┐
            │        Carding          │
            └─────────────────────────┘
                         │
                         ▼
            ┌─────────────────────────┐
            │        Drawing          │
            └─────────────────────────┘
                    ╱         ╲
                   ▼           ▼
    ┌──────────────────┐  ┌──────────────────┐
    │ Open End Spinning │  │   Ring Spinning  │
    └──────────────────┘  └──────────────────┘
                   ╲           ╱
                    ▼         ▼
            ┌─────────────────────────┐
            │        Weaving          │
            └─────────────────────────┘
                    ╱         ╲
                   ▼           ▼
    ┌──────────────────┐  ┌──────────────────┐
    │   Rope Dyeing    │  │   Seed Dyeing    │
    └──────────────────┘  └──────────────────┘
                   ╲           ╱
                    ▼         ▼
            ┌─────────────────────────┐
            │       Finishing         │
            └─────────────────────────┘
```

1. **Opening and Blending**- Opening begins with baled cotton fiber being separated into small tufts. A blend of cotton fibers is made on each opening line. These bales are selected using USDA High Volume Instrument (HVI) data***, and computer blending software produces optimal yarn strength.

2. **Carding**- Cotton is delivered by air suction from the Opening and Blending lines, through additional cleaning and blending machines, to the Cards. The major functions of Carding are to remove foreign matter and short fibers, form the cotton into a web and convert the web into a rope-like form known as a sliver.

3. **Drawing**- The drawing process produces a single, uniform sliver from six card slivers. The additional blending, paralleling of fibers and cleaning in this process produces a sliver for Open End and Ring Spinning.

4. **Spinning**- There are two spinning techniques. Open End Spinning and Ring Spinning.
   - **Open End Spinning**- Cotton Fibers are formed into a yarn by centrifugal action in Open- End Spinning. Individual fibers are laid down in the groove of a fast spinning rotor and twisted into yarn. The Open End Spinning Machines have robots on each side which automatically pieces up (repairs broken ends). On a different track, they have another robot that automatically doffs (removes full packages) and starts up a new package.

   - **Ring Spinning**- in Ring Spinning, the spinning frames receives Roving via a transit system from the roving machine. Yarn is formed from cotton fibers that are twisted together after being drafted by passing between three steel rolls and three rubber rolls. The yarn then is wrapped on a bobbin as it spins on a spindle by use of a

traveler. The relationship between roll speeds, traveler speeds and spindle speeds controls the amount of twist in the yarn.

Ring Spinning

Ring Spinning

After the cotton fibers are spun into yarn, the yarn is wound into a large package.

5. **Dying Process (Warp Preparation) –**
   ROPE DYEING
   The classical rope dyeing system is very labor intensive and consists of:
   - Ball warping
   - Indigo dyeing
   - Rebeaming on long- chain-beamer
   - Sizing

A warper ball

Indigo dying

Yarn from the ring spinning machine is wound on automatic winding machines on to a suitable package either cylindrical or 5057 cone. The winders are directly linked to the ring spinning frames and the cops joint by splicing. OE yarns are directly reeled up on the Ball warper.

The required No. of ends (usually 380 – 420 ends) are assembled into a rope. These ends are wound onto a core. The rope is guided similar as a cross wound package and wound into a ball, length of ball approx. 12 – 15.000 meters.

A lease is inserted at the start and end of the rope. The facilitate Rebeaming every 1000 meters an additional lease is inserted. Usually 18 – 24 ropes are simultaneously process on the rope dyeing machine. Prior to dyeing, the ropes are boiled out and treated with caustic-soda and wetting agent to remove from the cotton oil, impurities which could influence the fastness for the dye.

To dye with indigo, the ropes are immersed into the dye-bath. To dye in rope 30 – 60 seconds immersion (20 meters yarn) and 60 - 180 seconds are required for the oxidation of the Indigo dyestuff to ensure that also ends in the centre of the rope are equally dyed. Please note that squeezing pressure is important- 5 tons- as fastness of color and shade depends on even squeezing pressure. The comparatively long immersion and oxidation time requires a comparatively expensive equipment of machinery.

In order to obtain the required deep shade of blue color the ropes are immersed 5 – 6 times in a sequence of dye boxes with an oxidation range - so called skying - after each dye box. (Indigo belongs to the group of the vat dyes which is water-soluble in reduced solution and becomes an insoluble pigment when oxidized.

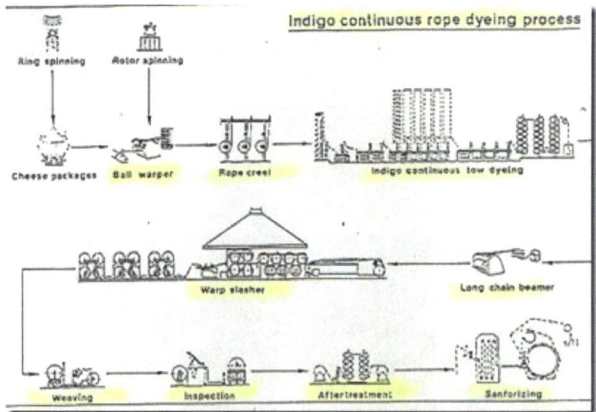

Having passed the dyeing and oxidation rage the ropes are guided through 2 or 3 washing boxes to wash off excessive dye .In the last box softener are added to ease the opening of the ropes. They are dried in a series of cans. The dried ropes which contain 380 – 420 ends are then deposited into large coilers .Rebeaming with 300 – 380 ends per rope is easier. These coilers are placed behind the long chain beamer where the Rebeaming and opening of the ropes takes place. In order to guarantee even yarn tension through Rebeaming on to a back beam ready for sizing the ropes are guided over a tension device which is placed approx. 10 -11 meters distance from the long chain beamer. Broken ends which very really happen during process of the rope

dyeing are repaired at this process stage. Initially these machines were supplied without yarn stop motion but are available now-a-days on special request. This is of major importance as lost ends, fluff, 3 – tail ends and yarn remnants can cause inferior performance in weaving.

Slashing coats the yarn with a starch/wax solution

The so prepared beck beams are now sized in a sizing machine preferably with 2 size boxes. The size pick up varies between 8 – 10%. In Europe mainly modified starches with binders are used, whilst in USA certain low % of PVA is applied in combination with starches by some companies. Depending on the final finishing process (washed denim) with no filler also CMC gives excellent performance in weaving. Special size mixes for soft denim will be discussed separately. We recommend however not to use PVA for sizing of denim as a surface of denim may show a leather skinned appearance.

6. **Weaving**- The weaving process interlaces the warp, which are the length-wise indigo dyed yarn and the filling, which are the natural-colored cross-wise yarn. The warp thread is in the form of sheet. The weft thread is inserted between two layers of warp sheets by means of a suitable carrier, such as Shuttle***, Projectile***, Rapier***, Air current, Water current, etc. The selection of carrier depends upon the type of weaving machinery used. The two different technologies available for weaving machines are - Conventional Shuttle Weaving System which is done by Ordinary Looms or Automatic Looms; and the Shuttle less Weaving System which is done by Airjet, Waterjet, Rapier, or a Projectile weaving machine. The Conventional Shuttle loom results in lesser production due to slow speed and excessive wear and tear of machinery. As such, now denim is generally woven through Shuttle less Weaving System namely, Airjet looms, rapier looms or projectile looms.

In a twill weave, each weft or filling yarn floats across the warp yarns in a progression of interlacings to the right or left, forming a distinct diagonal line. This is called a Right Hand Twill or a Left Hand Twill respectively.

Right and Left hand twill

Twill weave is often designated as a fraction—such as 2/1—in which the numerator indicates the number of harnesses that are raised (and, thus, threads crossed), in this example, two, and the denominator indicates the number of harnesses that are lowered when a filling yarn is inserted, in this example one. The fraction 2/1 would be read as "two up, one down." The minimum number of harnesses needed to produce a twill can be determined by totaling the numbers in the fraction. For the example described, the number of harnesses is three. Examples of warp faced twills are 2/1, 3/1, 4/1, 5/1 etc. Most denims have been traditionally 3/1 weaves, though lighter weight denims (under 10.5 ounces/sqare yard) often use the 2/1 configuration.

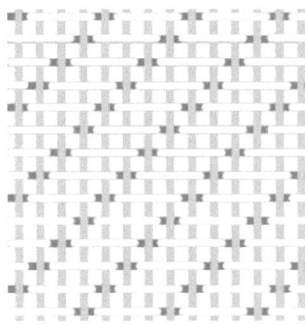

3/1 twill weave

7. **Finishing**- The final woven fabric, wound on a cloth roll, is taken out from weaving machines at particular intervals and checked on inspection machines so that any possible weaving fault can be detected. In this quality control exercise, wherever any fault is seen, corrective measures are taken then and there only. The woven Denim Fabrics then goes through various finishing processes, such as brushing, singeing, washing, impregnation for dressing and drying. Brushing and singeing eliminate impurities and help to even the surface of denim fabric. Dressing regulates the hand and rigidity of the fabric while compressive shrinking manages its dimensional stability. The standard width denim fabrics are then sent for making up. In this

process, the fabric is cut into the desired width according to the size required. The made- up denim fabric is then thoroughly checked for defects such as weaving defects, uneven dyeing, bleaching and dyeing defects, oil stains, or patches. After inspection, the final product is categorized quality-wise. The fault less fabrics are sent to the packaging department while the defective ones are sent for further corrections.

Woven denim entering the finishing range

A view of denim being singed

Source- http://www.pcca.com/Services/Denim/ManufacturingProcess.asp
http://www.teonline.com/knowledge-centre/manufacturing-process-denim.html
http://textilepedia.blogspot.com/2009/03/dyeing-process-for-denim-rope-dyeing.html
http://www.denimsandjeans.com/denim/manufacturing-process/indigo-dyeing-%E2%80%93-various-methods-explained-and-compared/

OPERATIONAL BREAKDOWN OF DENIM MANUFACTURING

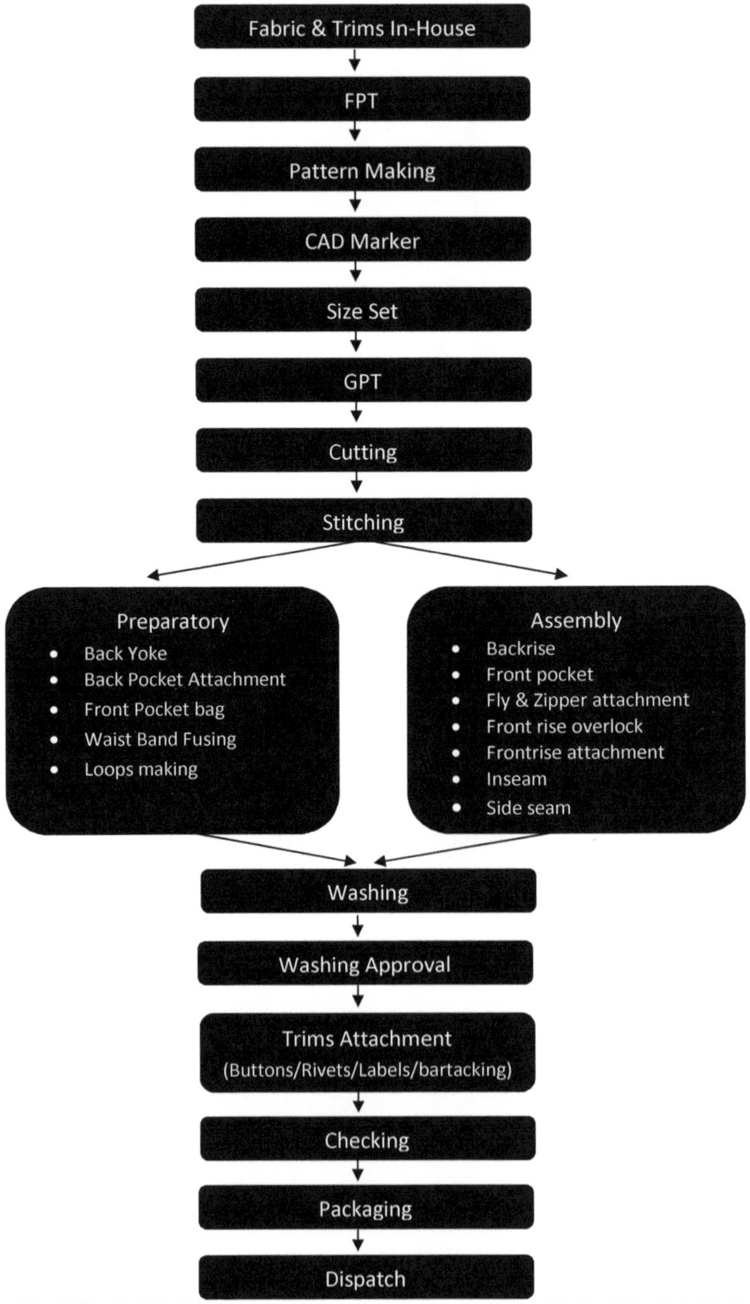

Fabric & Trims In-House
↓
FPT
↓
Pattern Making
↓
CAD Marker
↓
Size Set
↓
GPT
↓
Cutting
↓
Stitching

Preparatory
- Back Yoke
- Back Pocket Attachment
- Front Pocket bag
- Waist Band Fusing
- Loops making

Assembly
- Backrise
- Front pocket
- Fly & Zipper attachment
- Front rise overlock
- Frontrise attachment
- Inseam
- Side seam

Washing
↓
Washing Approval
↓
Trims Attachment
(Buttons/Rivets/Labels/bartacking)
↓
Checking
↓
Packaging
↓
Dispatch

Cost breakdown (Components)

1. Fabric
2. Cutting
3. Thread
4. Stitching
5. Fusing
6. Button
7. Zipper
8. Trim Fabric (Pocket bag/ waistband)
9. Labels (Washcare, size, brand)
10. Rivets
11. Brand Tag
12. Packaging items

Source - **Induro Lifestyle Resources Pvt. Ltd**
    # 93/1-2, Singasandra
    Hosur Highway
    Bangalore- 560008

DENIM LAUNDRY

In the 'Denim Industry', a Laundry is a manufacturing company that takes unwashed jeans and processes them. This processing includes washing, stone washing, sandblasting, garment dyeing, finishing, use of machine with abrasive bristles, applying enzymes to simulate a 'whisker' effect and sandpapering by hand. Laundries today are critical in making jeans look commercial and wash development has become as important as fabric development in the denim industry.

The denim Laundry Process can mainly be divided into two categories:-

- Dry Process (Part 1 and 2)
- Wet Process (Part 1and 2)

The basic breakdown of the laundry processes are as follows:-

1. **Dry Process Part 1 -**
   - Resin Spray and Woven Cure
   - Whiskering
   - Hand Brushing/ Scraping
   - Pinching

2. **Wet Process Part 1-**
   - Desizing
   - Rinse/ Dark Stone/ Mid Stone/Super Stone

3. **Dry Process Part 2-**
   - Grinding
   - Potassium Permanganate Spray (PP Spray)

4. **Wet Process Part 2-**
   - PP Spray neutralization
   - Softening
   - Tinting
   - Hydro Extraction
   - Tumble Dry

Edge Grinding

Whiskers

Chevron

PP Spray

Damaging/ Grinding

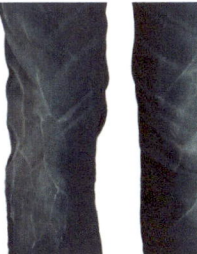 

Loop Tie

3D Crumple

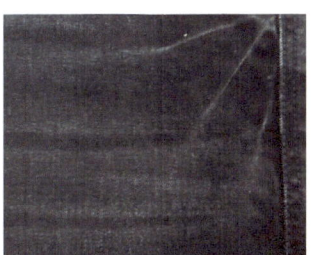

Acid washed jeans

Pinching/ Tagging

DRY PROCESS PART 1

WHISKERING/ CHEVERON

A fading of the ridges increases in the crotch area and back of the knees, which gives the appearance of aged denim. It can also be inverse- dark creased in faded denim.

This is the first step in the dry process. The stitched denim is sent to the whiskering unit, where the denims are put on the brushing mannequins. The denims are then either marked by chalk as to where the where the chevrons or whiskers are to be placed or they have template made which they place under the denim. They are then are rubbed by emery paper till the desired look is required. This is a complete manual work and the right look is achieved after years of experience.

Emery paper – It is the paper used to fade out the indigo from the denims. The gauge of the paper ranges from 200 to 400. Higher the gauge, softer the paper.

BRUSHING

Brushing is the fading of denims on the thigh and below area by brushing the garment with emery paper for a certain period of time. This scrapes out the indigo from those areas and gives a washed down look to the denim

PINCHING

Pinching is the process of tagging various parts the garment with a tag gun, so that that area remains unwashed, hence, creating a dark -light look. Usually done on the waist band or the edge of the front pockets at the side seam.

WET PROCESS PART 1

DESIZING

Desizing is the process of removing the starch content from the denim. This is done by using

- desizing agent,
- anti- backstainers (to avoid absorbency of the washed out indigo on to the denim),
- wetting agent (to help increase the absorbency of water)
- lubricators(to avoid friction between denims so that there are no random patterns made on the denims due to rubbing against each other)

The above mentioned ingredients are put in the washing machines with the denims at a temperature of 60°C, 1:6 water ratios for approximately 30 minutes.

After the desizing bath, the denims are given for **water wash**, to remove all the agents from the denims.

ENZYME PROCESS

There are two kinds of enzyme processes, Acid Cellulose, Neutral Cellulose and stoning.

Acid Cellulose

It works best in the pH value of 5.5 and exhibits optimum activity at a temperature of 55°C, the water ratio of 1:5 for a duration of 15-20 minutes.

Neutral Cellulose

it works best at a pH value of 6 and exhibits optimum activity at a temperature of 50°C. If the temperature increases, the enzymes stop working, hence temperature is a crucial point here.

Stoning

It is a cold process. In this they put pumice stones with water and denim and are washed.

Pumice Stones- Volcanic stone used for stone washing garments. Pumice is popular because of its strength and light weight. There are two kinds of Pumice stones, Indonesian Pumice and Turkey Pumice.

Turkey Pumice is preferred by most laundries as they are white in color and much more light weight then Indonesian pumice stones. Moreover, Indonesian Pumices are dark in color and hence, can't be used with light color denims.

After the enzyme bath is done, the denims are given **a water wash**.

Soda Soaping Process - It is a cleaning process which removes the indigo that is accumulated at the surface of the denim. It is done at a temperature of 60°C for about 10 minutes.

RINSE/ DARK STONE/ MID STONE/ SUPER STONE

Rinse level

This is the darkest level of wash in denims. The denims are put into the washing machine with anti-backstainers, lubricants and wetting agents at a temperature of 60°C for 5- 10 minutes and the rinse level is achieved.

Dark Stone

Dark stone level is achieved with the enzyme process which is mentioned above. But the time duration is a little longer.

Mid Stone

It is achieved with the chlorine (bleach) process. Bleach amount used to receive these levels ranges from 10-20 liters of bleach, run for 5-15 minutes depending on the level of wash required.

Super Stone

It is achieved with the chlorine (bleach) process. Bleach amount used to receive these levels ranges from 30-40 liters of bleach, run for about 40 minutes depending on the level of wash required.

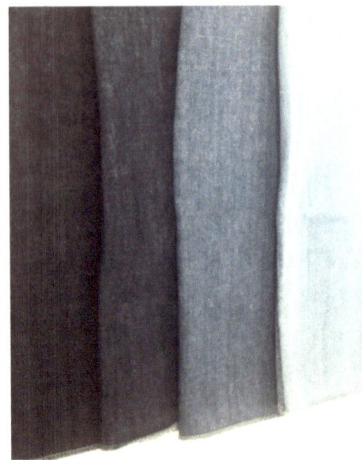

Rinse Level to Super Stone Level.
Left to Right

Ice wash

It is achieved with the chlorine (bleach) process. Bleach amount used to receive these levels are about 100 liters of bleach, run for about 45-50 minutes depending on the level of wash required.

After the bleach process it goes for a **water wash.**

After this process it goes for a **hydro peroxide wash**, which kills the bleaching agent. This process is done because if not done, the garment has a tendency to turn yellow when interacted with the natural atmosphere.

DRY PROCESS PART 2

GRINDING

This process is done to give a torn / work out look to the denim. There are two kinds of grinding machines, Hand Grinder and Bench grinder.

Hand grinder is used on the surface of the denim, whereas, bench grinder is used for the edes of the denim, like the pocket edge and the bottom hem.

POTASSIUM PERMANGANATE SPRAY (PP SPRAY)

I n this process, the denim is sprayed with a gun containing potassium permanganate on the areas where the washed out look is required (the potassium permanganate eats ups the indigo on the areas applied). The outcome is like brushing, but the fade is more intense. Moreover, this process does less harm to the yarn.

The spray is purple in color, which when oxidized turns yellowish-green.

WET PROCESS PART 2

PP NEUTRALIZATION

In this process the PP sprayed garments are washed with various neutralizers which washes out the PP and gives the final washed out look to the denims.

SOFTENING

In this process the garments are rinsed with antiozonate softener, again, to prevent the yellowing of the garment and to prevent ozone fading by storage.

OTHER PROCESSES DONE ON DENIMS

ACID WASH

This process is done to give the indigo denims a washed out look. It is done on a semi- washed garment. A paste of titanium dioxide and chlorine is run in a washing machine with thermacol balls. One the paste gets attached to the thermacol balls, the denims are put in and washed for 30 minutes. This process also gives denims a puckering effect and creates high and lows on the stitched areas.

RESIN TREATED CRUMPLE/ 3D CRUMPLE/ KEBAB

The denims are crumpled in accordance to the style requirement. Then the garment is treated with a resin solution. Resin created a bonding between cellulose (yarns), which makes the denim stiff.

Curing- this is the baking of the treated fabric. During this drying process, the resin substance undergoes a chemical reaction and links molecules within the denim fibers, durably bonding them to one another. This holds the fabric structure in precisely the form it had at the time of baking.

Curing is a process of 40 minutes. 20 minutes each cycle. The denims are first put on the mannequins and passed through the curing oven. Once it is out, it is removed from mannequin and hung on a hook and passed through the oven again. Once it is out. The denim holds its crumpled look.

LOOP TIE

In this process, the denim is tied up at various points, like in tie-dye process. But instead of it being dyes, it is washed. The areas which are tied remains dark and the remaining area gets washed out, hence giving the denim a different pattern.

NET TIE

In this process the garment is twisted and put into a net (it is an export quality stretchable net, which costs 30-40 Rs per meter) and then knotted at both ends. It is then sent for washing. The outcome of this process is random fading is slashes in various directions.

Source

Arvind Fashion Limited.

No. 12, 4th Cross
Bommasandra Industrial Area,
Bangalore- 560099

Laundry Capacity -	8000 denims per day
	800-1000 non-denims per day
Daily Output -	5000 denims + non-denims per day
Brands -	Lee, Wrangler, Excalibur Gant, U.S.A. 1949, Flying Machine, Energie', USPA, Izod, Arrow and many other export brands.

THE WASH COMPARISION PROCESS

Identification of three fabric sorts which are being used season on season in denims– to develop wash references in the same.

I chose three fabric sorts which are used in the staple styles every season and experimented with washes on it so that these sorts could also possibly be incorporated in the fashion styles in the future. The three Fabric sorts are :- PD 2072 (Blue), Merc Black and Jet Black. Once the fabric sorts were decided, I proceeded on to getting the leg mocks developed, to develop the washing references in the same. I requested for 12 leg mocks in each sort, leaving both laundries with 6 leg mocks each sort.

Researching on washes reference for the leg mocks development

I went through various denim brands and went through their washes and selected washes which would go well with Lee and which could be improvised upon to develop new washes. The washes were selected keeping in mind that the washes should be new as this will help us understand how well the laundries can grasp the technique and develop the closest reference to it. Once the washes were sorted I revised the designs so that they are apt for Lee.

Meeting with the laundry's wash development personnel

We had finalized on two laundries, Ramdhan and Chaitanya, which are our best laundires in Bangalore.

Once the pictures were decided I had to take the leg mocks to the laundry (Ramdhan) and meeting with the wash development personnel showing them the pictures, and the sorts, explaining my requirements and discussing the possibilities of achieving which look in which sort. I also assigned which washes were to be developed on which sort and leg mocks. This whole process went down with the first laundry and each leg mock was assigned a wash.

Going to the second laundry (Chaitanya) got easier, as all the leg mocks were already assigned with the washes. All I had to do was go there and tell them exactly what I need , as I had it all cleared out with the previous laundry and my motive was to ask them to follow the same wash directions as given to Ramdan, as this would be the most ideal situation for a comparative study.

Reviewing the washed samples and asking for improvisation according to the requirements

Once the washed legmocks started flowing in, I had to review them and ask them to re-do certain washed as the outcome was not right. This did not take a lot of time as most of the leg mocks reached a satisfactory level, also, due to the time constraint I could not go excessively overboard about the accuracies.

Developing the cost sheet of each leg mock

Once the leg mocks were in, I took the routing and developed the costing sheet of each leg mock in accordance to the standard price that is charged to Lee. This was to help me understand the cost difference in each laundry for the same process.

Visual analysis of the leg mocks

Once all the leg mocks were in from both the laundries I had to see which laundry had met with the requirements most closely in reference to the pictures and my needs and record it.

RAMDAN

CHAITANYA

RAMDAN

CHAITANYA

RAMDAN   **CHAITANYA**

COMPARATIVE COST ANALYSIS

RAMDHAN   **CHAITANYA**

Sort Name   **Merc Black**

No- 13	Wash Details	Cost
	Whisker	12
	Chevron	4
	Scrapping	12
	DS Wash	25
	Nicking	12
	PP Spray	13
	PP Bleach	
	Total	

No- 14	Wash Details	Cost
	Whisker	12
	Chevron	4
	Scrapping	12
	DS Wash	25
	Nicking	12
	PP Spray	13
	Total	**78**

No- 15	Wash Details	Cost
	Whisker	12
	Chevron	4
	Scrapping	12
	DS Wash	25
	Nicking	12
	PP Spray	13
	Final Iron Crumple	
	Total	

No- 1	Wash Details	Cost
	Whisker	10
	Chevron	3
	Scrapping	10
	DS Wash	23
	PP Spray	11
	Total	**57**

No- 2	Wash Details	Cost
	Whisker	10
	Chevron	3
	Scrapping	10
	DS Wash	23
	Nicking	10
	PP Spray	11
	Bleach	
	Total	

No- 3	Wash Details	Cost
	Whisker	10
	Chevron	3
	Scrapping	10
	DS Wash	23
	Nicking	10
	PP Spray	11
	Final Iron Crumple	
	Tint	8
	Total	

No- 16	Wash Details	Cost
	Whisker	12
	Chevron	4
	Scrapping	12
	DS Wash	25
	PP Spray	13
	Total	**66**

No- 17	Wash Details	Cost
	Whisker	12
	Chevron	4
	Scrapping	12
	DS Wash	25
	PP Spray	13
	Tie Effect	15
	Total	**81**

No- 4	Wash Details	Cost
	Whisker	10
	Chevron	3
	Scrapping	10
	DS Wash	23
	PP Spray	11
	Tie Effect	13
	Total	**70**

No- 5	Wash Details	Cost
	Whisker	10
	Chevron	3
	Scrapping	10
	DS Wash	23
	PP Spray	11
	Total	**57**

RAMDHAN   **CHAITANYA**

Sort Name   **Jet Black**

No- 1	Wash Details	Cost
	Whisker	12
	Chevron	4
	Scrapping	12
	DS Wash	25
	PP Spray	13
	Total	**66**

No- 2	Wash Details	Cost
	Whisker	12
	Chevron	4
	Scrapping	12
	DS Wash	25
	PP Spray	13
	Back Knee Whisker	10
	Total	**76**

No- 3	Wash Details	Cost
	Resin Spray	15
	Kebab	25
	Scrapping	12
	Tie Effect	15
	DS Wash	25
	PP Spray	13
	Total	**105**

No- 1	Wash Details	Cost
	Nicking	10
	Whisker	10
	Chevron	3
	Scrapping	10
	DS Wash	23
	PP Spray	11
	Total	**67**

No- 2	Wash Details	Cost
	Whisker	10
	Chevron	3
	Scrapping	10
	DS Wash	23
	PP Spray	11
	Nicking	10
	Total	**67**

No- 3	Wash Details	Cost
	Nicking	10
	Whisker	10
	Chevron	3
	Scrapping	10
	Tie Effect	13
	DS Wash	23
	PP Spray	11
	Total	**80**

No- 4	Wash Details	Cost
	Resin Spray	15
	Kebab	25
	Scrapping	12
	Tie Effect	15
	DS Wash	25
	PP Spray	13
	Chevron	4
	Total	**109**

No- 4	Wash Details	Cost
	Resin Spray	13
	Kebab	23
	Scrapping	10
	Tie Effect	13
	DS Wash	23
	PP Spray	11
	Chevron	3
	Total	**96**

No- 5	Wash Details	Cost
	Whisker	12
	Chevron	4
	Scrapping	12
	DS Wash	25
	PP Spray	13
	Tagging	6
	Total	**72**

No- 5	Wash Details	Cost
	Whisker	10
	Chevron	3
	Scrapping	10
	DS Wash	23
	PP Spray	11
	Tagging	4
	Total	**61**

RAMDHAN   **CHAITANYA**

Sort Name   **PD- 2072**

No- 1	Wash Details	Cost
	Resin Spray	15
	Curing	5
	Chevron	4
	Scrapping	12
	DS Wash	25
	PP Spray	15
	Final Color Spray	
	Total	**76**

No- 1	Wash Details	Cost
	Resin Spray	13
	Curing	3
	Chevron	3
	Scrapping	10
	DS Wash	23
	PP Spray	13
	Total	

No- 2	Wash Details	Cost
	Whisker	12
	Chevron	4
	Scrapping	12
	MS Wash	32
	Towel Bleach	
	Nicking	12
	PP Spray	13
	Total	

No- 2	Wash Details	Cost
	Whisker	10
	Chevron	3
	Scrapping	10
	MS Wash	30
	Nicking	10
	PP Spray	11
	Total	**74**

No- 3	Wash Details	Cost
	Resin Spray	15
	Kebab	25
	Curing	5
	Merging	10
	DS Wash	25
	Grinding	6
	Nicking	12
	PP Spray	13
	Total	**111**

No- 3	Wash Details	Cost
	Resin Spray	13
	Kebab	23
	Curing	3
	Merging	8
	DS Wash	23
	Nicking	10
	PP Spray	11
	Total	**91**

No- 4	Wash Details	Cost
	Resin Spray	15
	Kebab	25
	Curing	5
	Chevron	4
	MS Wash	32
	Grinding	6
	Nicking	12
	PP Spray	13
	Tinting	10
	Total	**122**

No- 4	Wash Details	Cost
	Resin Spray	13
	Kebab	23
	Curing	3
	Chevron	3
	MS Wash	30
	Nicking	10
	PP Spray	11
	Total	**93**

No- 5	Wash Details	Cost
	Whisker	12
	Chevron	4
	Scrapping	12
	MS Wash	32
	Towel Bleach	
	Grinding	6
	Nicking	12
	PP Spray	13
	Tinting	10
	Total	

No- 5	Wash Details	Cost
	Whisker	10
	Chevron	3
	Scrapping	10
	MS Wash	30
	Nicking	10
	PP Spray	11
	Tinting	8
	Total	**82**

No- 6	Wash Details	Cost
	Whisker	12
	Chevron	4
	Scrapping	12
	MS Wash	32
	Grinding	6
	Nicking	12
	PP Spray	13
	Tinting	10
	Total	**101**

No- 6	Wash Details	Cost
	Whisker	10
	Chevron	3
	Scrapping	10
	MS Wash	30
	Nicking	10
	PP Spray	11
	Tinting	8
	Total	**82**

FINDINGS/ CONCLUSIONS/ RECOMMENDATIONS

Visual analysis

Ramdhan has a better grasp of techniques that could be applied to our fashion styles, but they lack precision.
Chaitanya, whereas does not have that wide a facility or knowledge of new techniques that are being done in the market, but they do everything with great precision as far as simples styles matter.

Cost Effectiveness

The cost of the washes in Ramdhan is comparatively much higher than that of Chaitanya. Each and every process has an average difference of 2 Rs. and a wholesome difference of 10 Rs. at an average per denim.

Recommendations

I suggest that we give our new, experimental and complicated fashion styles to Ramdhan, this will help us achieve our required look very closely, the price will be higher in comparison to Chaitanya, but will also get the output. We could give comparatively simpler fashion styles and staples to Chaitanya, they will be able to achieve the required look well and we would also get a better price for it. This distribution will balance out the overall costing of denims.

COMPETITIVE FIT MAPPING FOR WOMENS FITS AND NEW DEVELOPMENTS

The aim of the fit study is to study the current women fits available in Lee and the competitive brands. Find the difference in the fits and develop a competitive fit chart, which would help us analyze what are the new fits that the competitors are experimenting with and see where we are lacking. Also, conduct a survey to know women's views and problems faced when it comes to jeans. After the analysis, suggest new fits that could be incorporated in Lee.

DIRECTIONS FOR MEASUREMENT

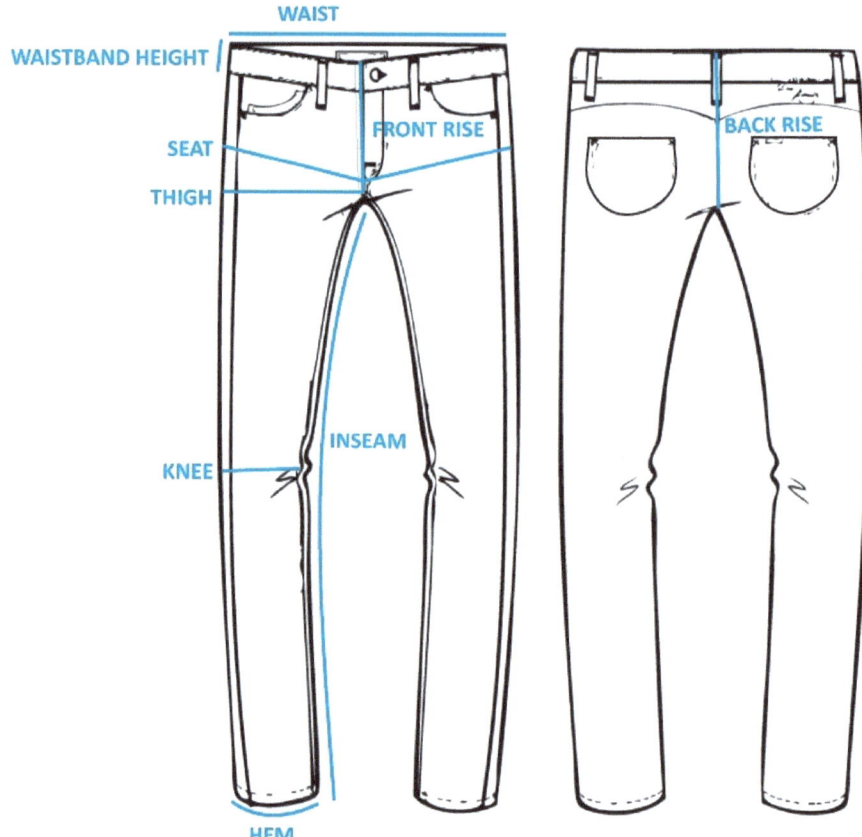

Waist- The girth of the garment at the top edge of the waistband.

Waistband Height- The height of the waistband from the tip of the garment to the end of the waistband.

Front Rise- The height of the center front of the garment from the tip of the waist band till the front and back panel intersection at the crotch.

Back Rise- The height of the center back of the garment from the tip of the waistband to the intersection point of the front and the back panel.

Seat- The horizontal measurement of the garment immediately below the J stitch.

Thigh- The girth of the leg panel immediately below the crotch level.

Inseam- The height of the garment from the crotch intersection of both leg panels to the hem of the garment.

Knee- The girth of the garment at half of inseam minus 2.

Hem – The girth of the garment at the edge of the leg panel.

Step 1-

Analysis of the current fits available in Lee, namely, Eva, Roxy Maxi.

Size- 28   DIFFERENCE IN MEASUREMENTS IN THE THREE LEE FITS - EVA, ROXY, MAXI

	MEASURE POINTS	EVA	ROXY	MAXI	EVA-ROXY	EVA-MAXI	ROXY-MAXI
1	WAIST - Straight	29 1/2	30	30	- 1/2	- 1/2	0
2	SEAT -measure J stitch length from bottom of W.B at 3 points	4 1/8	3 3/4	2 3/4	3/8	1 3/8	1
3	SEAT -measure of W.B at 3 points	35	36	36	-1	-1	0
4	THIGH - at crotch level	21	21 1/4	21 1/4	- 1/4	- 1/4	0
5	KNEE-half inseam 2'' above	14 1/4	13 1/2	13	3/4	1 1/4	½
6	Bottom Hem Opening	13 1/2	12	10	1 1/2	3 1/2	2
7	F.RISE - including W.B	8 1/4	7 3/4	6 3/4	1/2	1 1/2	1
8	B. RISE - including W.B	12 3/4	13	11 3/4	- 1/4	1	1 ¼
9	J Stitch Length	4 1/2	4	3	1/2	1 1/2	1
10	Zipper Length	4	3.5	2 1/2	1/2	1 1/2	1

**The maximum differences are highlighted in green

Step 2-

Studying the measurements of the fits available in the competitive brands, namely, Levis and Pepe Jeans.

Levi's

FIT NAME	Slight Curve		Demi Curve		Bold Curve	
Measurement Points	28	30	28	30	28	30
Waist	31 1/2	33 1/4	31	32 3/4	30	31 1/2
Front Rise (incl. W.B)	7 3/4	8	8	8 1/2	7 1/2	8
Back Rise (incl. W.B)	12 1/4	13	13	13 1/2	12 3/4	13 1/2
Seat	35 1/2	37 3/8	36	38	37 1/4	39 1/4
Thigh	20 1/2	21	21	21 1/2	22	23
Knee	14 1/2	14 3/4	14	14 1/4	14 3/4	15
Bottom Hem	12	12 1/2	12 1/2	13	12 1/2	13

Pepe Jeans

FIT NAME	Frisky		Pixie		Gina	
Measurement Points	28	30	28	30	28	30
Waist	30 1/2	32 1/4	31 1/2	33 1/4	29 1/2	31 1/4
Front Rise (incl. W.B)	7 1/2	8	6 1/2	7 1/4	9 1/2	9 3/4
Back Rise (incl. W.B)	11 3/4	12	11 1/4	11 3/4	12 3/4	13
Seat	34	37	33.5	36.5	35	38
Thigh	20	21	18 1/2	20	20 1/2	21 1/2
Knee	13 1/2	14	13	13 1/2	15 1/2	15 1/2
Bottom Hem	12	12	11	11.5	14 3/4	15

**The best sellers are highlighted in green

Step 3-

Do a comparative analysis on the fits available in all the three brands, namely, Lee, Levi's, and Pepe Jeans.

FIT NAME	ROXY	Demi Curve	Frisky
Waist	30	31	30 1/2
Front Rise (incl. W.B)	7 3/4	8	7 1/2
Back Rise (incl. W.B)	13	13	11 3/4
Seat	36	36	34
Thigh	21 1/4	21	20
Knee	13 1/2	14	13 1/2
Bottom Hem	12	12 1/2	12

FIT NAME	Pixie	MAXI
Waist	31 1/2	30
Front Rise (incl. W.B)	6 1/2	6 3/4
Back Rise (incl. W.B)	11 1/4	11 3/4
Seat	33.5	36
Thigh	18 1/2	21 1/4
Knee	13	13
Bottom Hem	11	10

FIT NAME	Gina	EVA
Waist	29 1/2	29 1/2
Front Rise (incl. W.B)	9 1/2	8 1/4
Back Rise (incl. W.B)	12 3/4	12 3/4
Seat	35	35
Thigh	20 1/2	21
Knee	15 1/2	14 1/4
Bottom Hem	14 3/4	13 1/2

FIT NAME	Bold Curve	Slight Curve
Waist	30	31 1/2
Front Rise (incl. W.B)	7 1/2	7 3/4
Back Rise (incl. W.B)	12 3/4	12 1/4
Seat	37 1/4	35 1/2
Thigh	22	20 1/2
Knee	14 3/4	14 1/2
Bottom Hem	12 1/2	12

The fits put together are the styles which are similar to each other.

- Roxy, Demi Curve and Frisky are similar styles and are also the best selling in Lee, Levi's and Pepe Jeans.
- Maxi and Pixie are the next best sellers in Lee and Pepe Jeans
- Eva and Gina are the least selling brands in Lee and Pepe Jeans respectively.
- Bold Curve and Slight Curve of Levi's do not match any of Lee or Pepe Jeans fit.

Conclusion

Most of the fits of Lee and Pepe jeans are the same.

Levi's is targeting a wider market by creating these new fits. *Slight Curve* targets women with flat bottoms where as *Bold Curve* targets women with big bottoms.

SAMPLE QUESTIONNAIRE

Hi, I am an Associate Professor at Modart International, New Delhi; I am conducting a survey as part of my research paper. I would be very grateful if you could take a little time out and fill in the questionnaire.

Age

☐ 15-20   ☐ 21-25   ☐ 26-30   ☐ 31-35   ☐ 36-40   ☐ 41 and above

Monthly Income

☐ Student   ☐ Unemployed   ☐ 0-15000   ☐ 16000- 25000   ☐ 26000- 35000

☐ 36000- 45000   ☐ 46000 and above

Waist

☐ 24   ☐ 26   ☐ 28   ☐ 30   ☐ 32   ☐ 34   ☐ 36   ☐ 38 and above

How frequently do you wear jeans?

☐ Every day   ☐ On Weekends   ☐ Once a week   ☐ Once a month   ☐ I don't wear them

Which factor influences your purchase in jeans? (Please rank from 1-7, *1 being the highest and 7 the lowest*)

☐ They are good quality and will last long   ☐ They are up-to-minute with fashion   ☐ They camouflage my flaws

☐ They make me look slimmer   ☐ Price is reasonable   ☐ I like the fit

☐ I like the brand

What outside factors influences your choice? (Please rank from 1-7, *1 being the highest and 7 the lowest*)

☐ Celebrity endorsement   ☐ Friends   ☐ Street fashion   ☐ Magazines   ☐ Movies

☐ Salesperson   ☐ Advertisements

Which brand are you most likely to own? (Please rank from 1-5, *1 being the highest and 5 the lowest*)

☐ Lee   ☐ Levis   ☐ Pepe Jeans   ☐ Wrangler   ☐ Non- branded

☐ Others (Please Specify) _____

How would you rank the following brands on the basis of :-

Their fits?   (Please rank from 1-4, *1 being the highest and 4 the lowest*)

☐ Lee   ☐ Levis   ☐ Pepe Jeans   ☐ Wrangler

Style updates with the changing fashion? (Please rank from 1-4, _1 being the highest and 4 the lowest_)

☐ Lee ☐ Levis ☐ Pepe Jeans ☐ Wrangler

Where do you usually wear your jeans?

☐ Work ☐ Parties ☐ Casual day out ☐ Home ☐ I don't wear them

Do your price points for buying jeans differ from occasion to occasion?

☐ Yes ☐ No ☐ Sometimes

How many pairs of jeans do you currently own?

☐ 1-3 ☐ 4-6 ☐ 7-9 ☐ 10-12

How many of these do you wear frequently?

☐ 1-2 ☐ 3-5 ☐ 6-8

What body type are you?

☐ Pear ☐ Hourglass ☐ Rectangle ☐ Inverse pear

It is very difficult to find a pair of jeans that fits perfectly

☐ I Agree ☐ I disagree ☐ I don't know

Have you ever bought men's jeans for yourself?

☐ Yes ☐ No

If yes, what was the reason for it?

☐ I could not find my size
☐ I preferred the collection they had for men's
☐ I was persuaded by the salesman to buy it
☐ Others (Please Specify)_____

What is the most common problem you face while buying jeans?

☐ Usually fit in the hips and thighs but are too tight in the waist

☐ Usually fit in the waist, but don't flatter my figure
☐ Fit in the hips and thighs, but gape at the back
☐ Others (Please Specify) _____

How many pairs of jeans do you usually try before buying one?

☐ 1-3   ☐ 4-6   ☐ 7-10

What kind of fit in jeans do you like?

☐ Loose/relaxed fit   ☐ Slim fit (defines the body shape)   ☐ Skinny (like a second skin)

Thank You! ☺

SURVEY RESULTS

I conducted a survey through the internet and through direct contact with women. The following graphs represent the responses from the women for each question

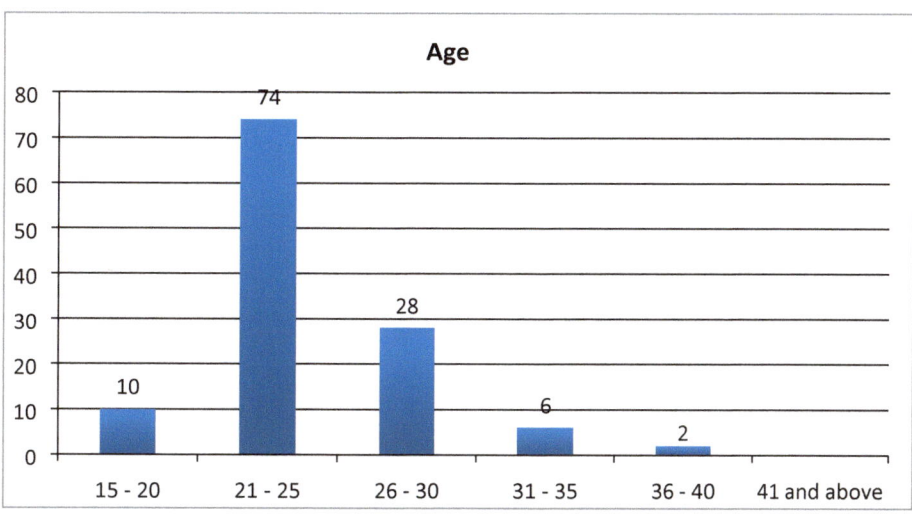

The age group of maximum of my respondents is between 21-25

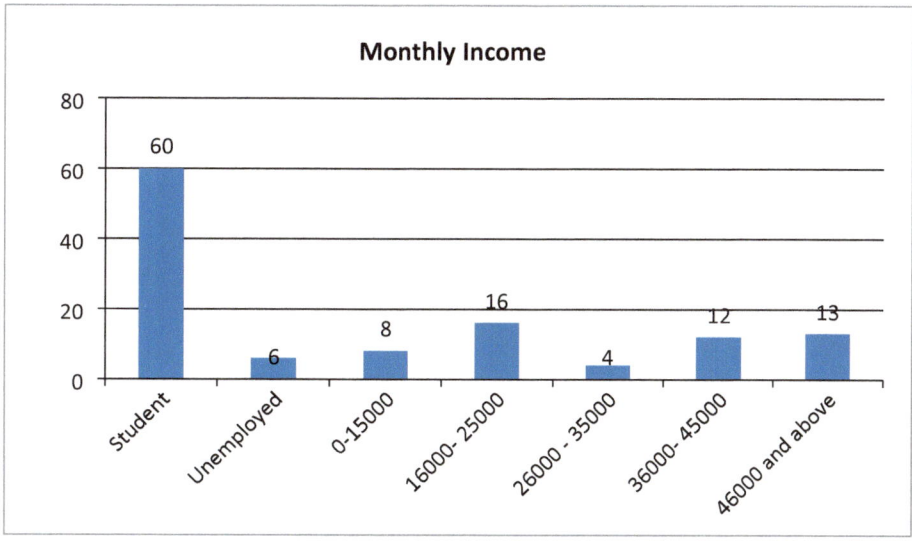

The maximum responses have come from students

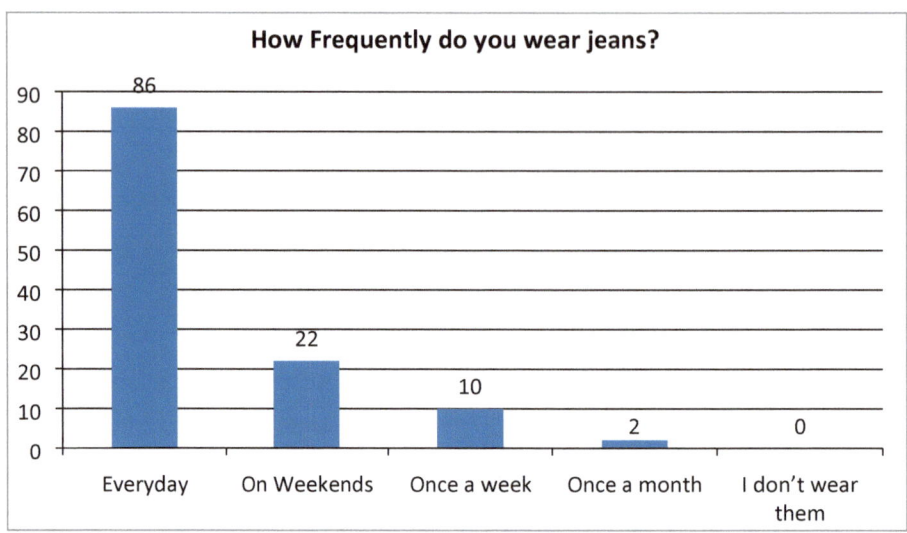

Most women wear jeans everyday or weekdays.

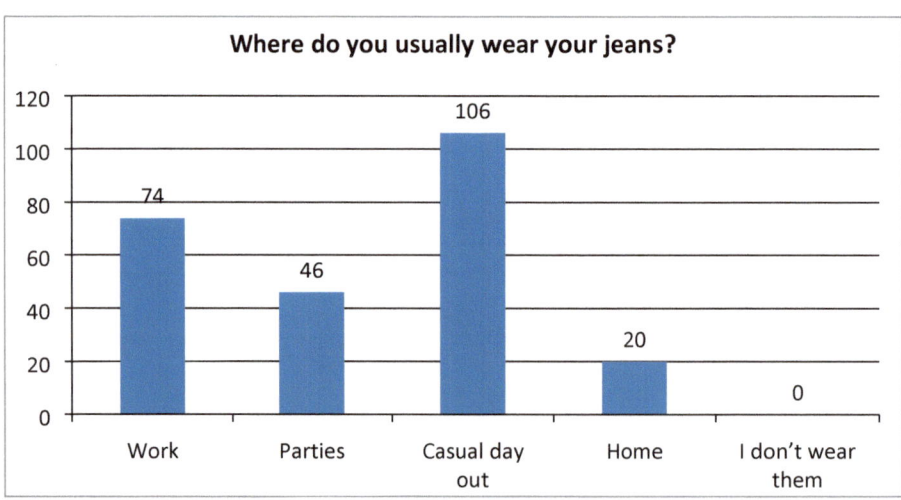

Jeans is still the garment for casual days.

Do your price point differ from occasion to occasion ?

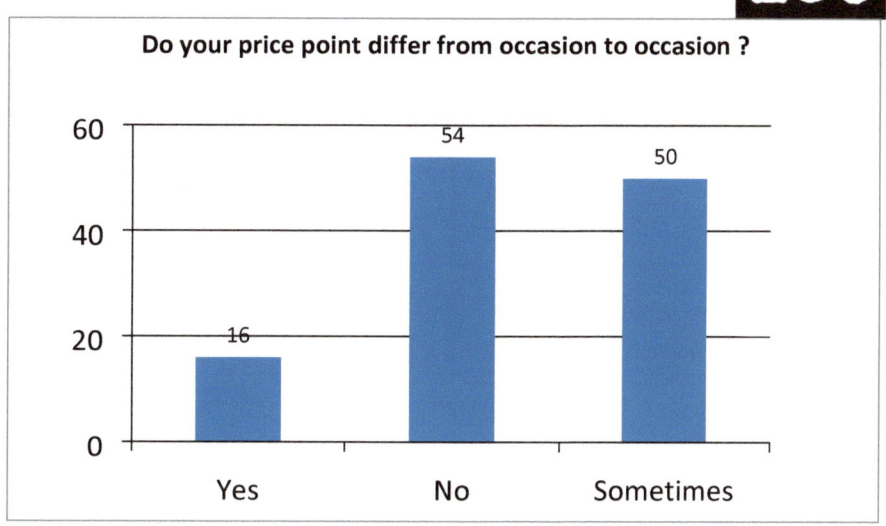

Maximum women said the price points do not differ for them while buying jeans

Where do you usually wear your jeans?

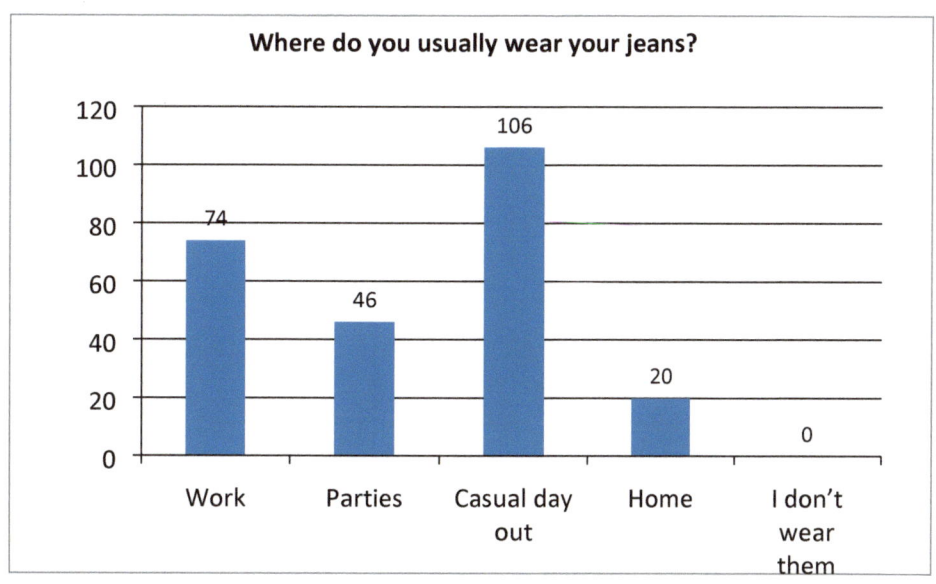

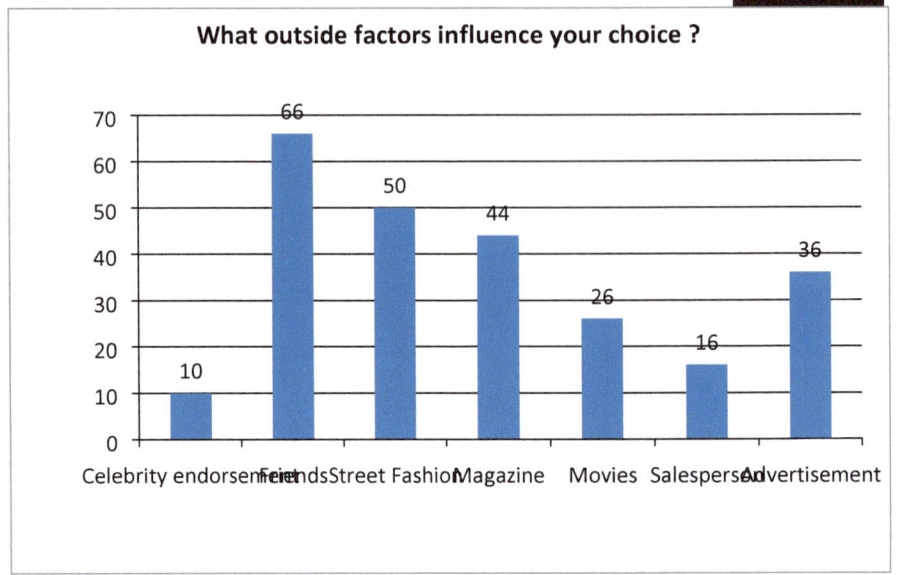

What outside factors influence your choice ?

Factor	Value
Celebrity endorsement	10
Friends	66
Street Fashion	50
Magazine	44
Movies	26
Salesperson	16
Advertisement	36

Which brand are you most likely to own? (1 being the highest and 6 the lowest)

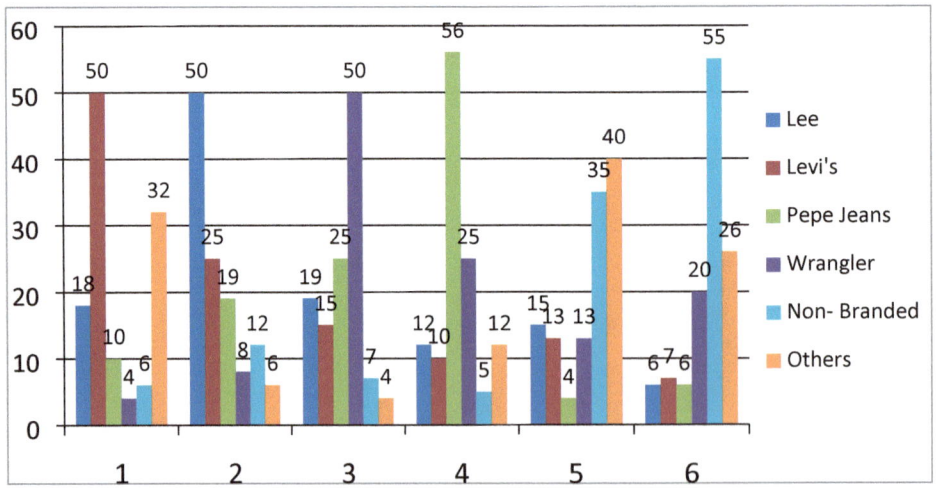

Legend: Lee, Levi's, Pepe Jeans, Wrangler, Non-Branded, Others

Others included brands like Mango, Zara, UniQLo, UCB, Alcott, Splash, Bare, Forever21, Max, X'pose and Sisley.

How would you rank the brands on the basis of :-
(1 being the highest and 4 the lowest)

Their Fits

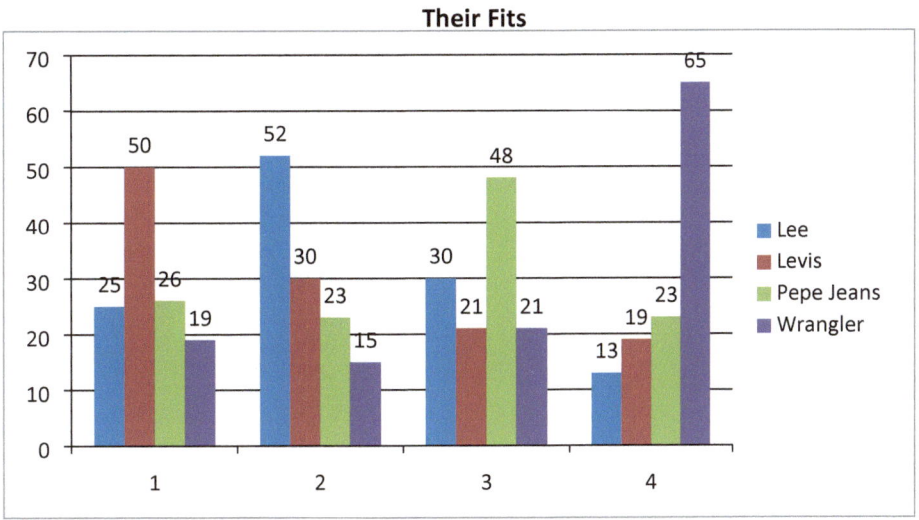

Style updates with changing fashion

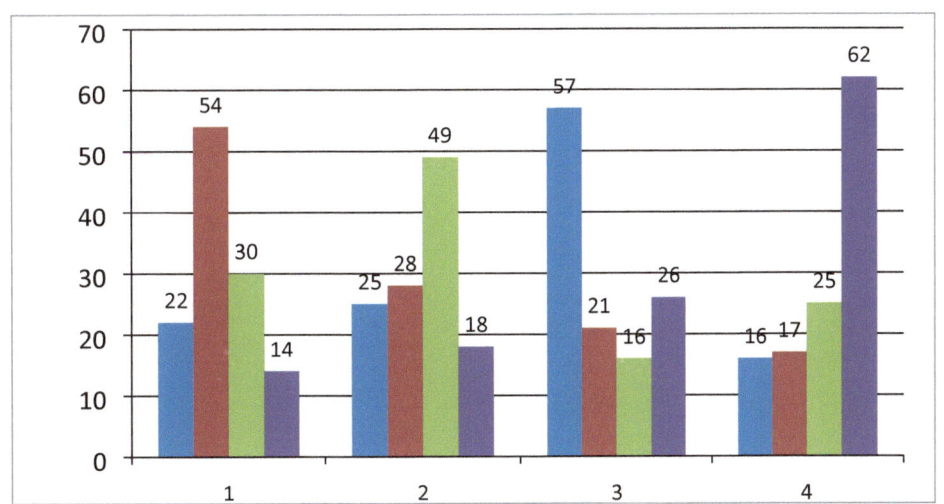

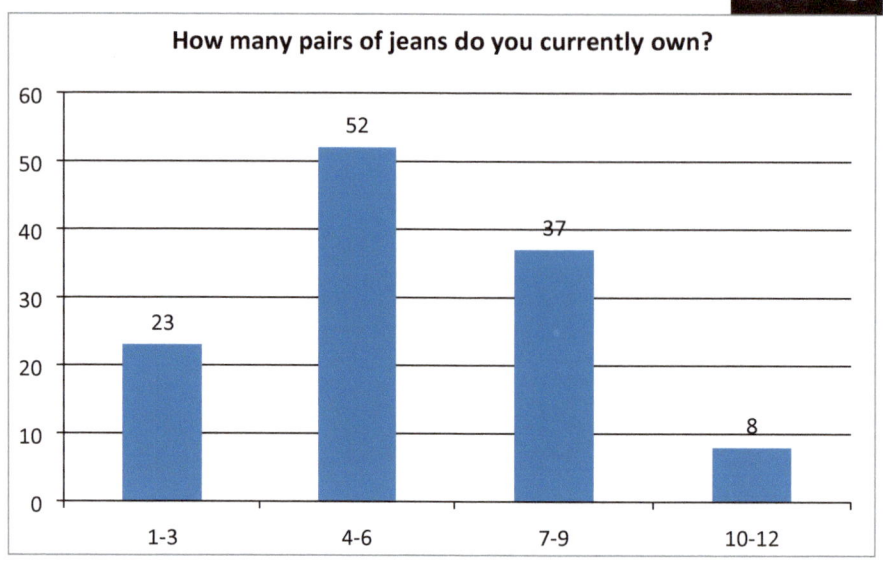

How many pairs of jeans do you currently own?

1-3	4-6	7-9	10-12
23	52	37	8

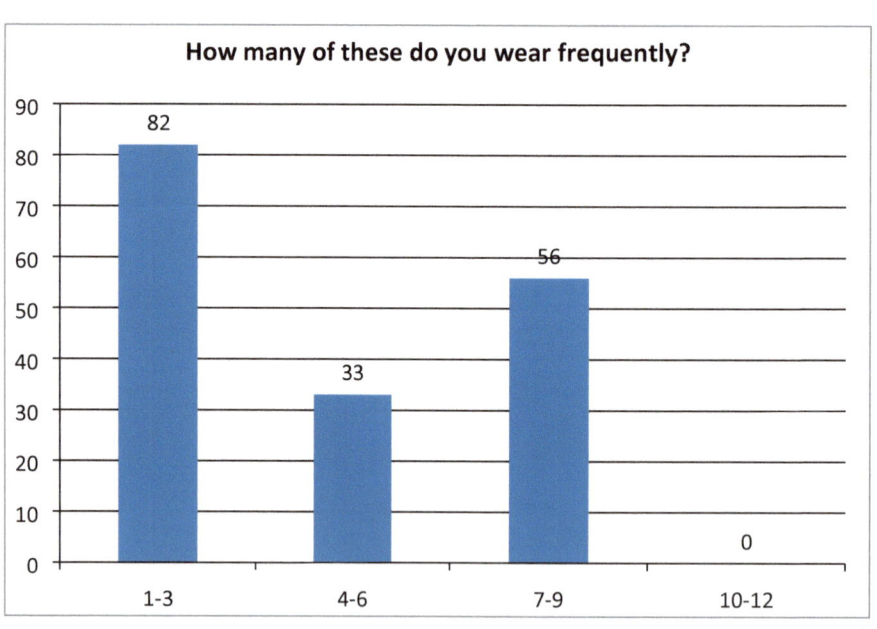

How many of these do you wear frequently?

1-3	4-6	7-9	10-12
82	33	56	0

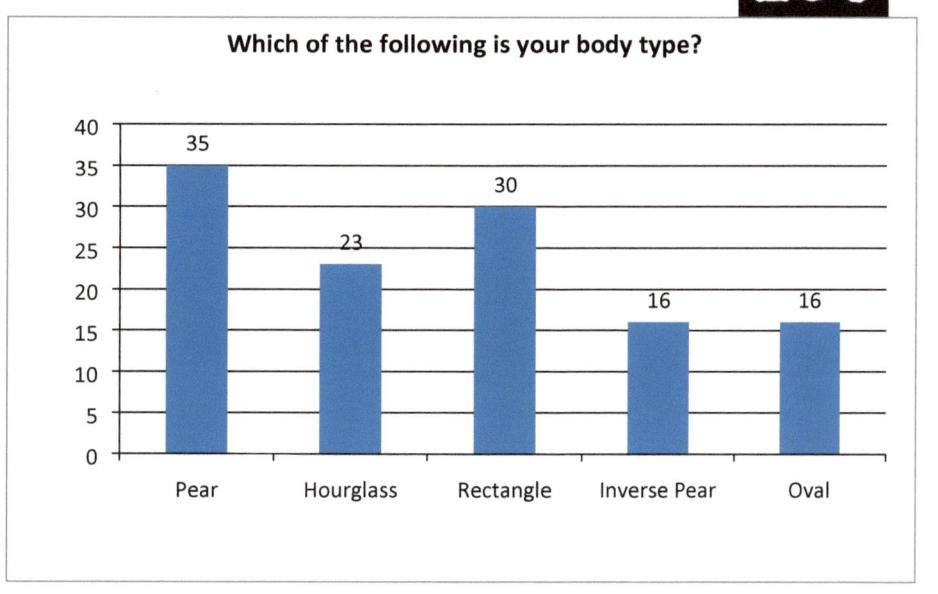

Which of the following is your body type?

Body Type	Value
Pear	35
Hourglass	23
Rectangle	30
Inverse Pear	16
Oval	16

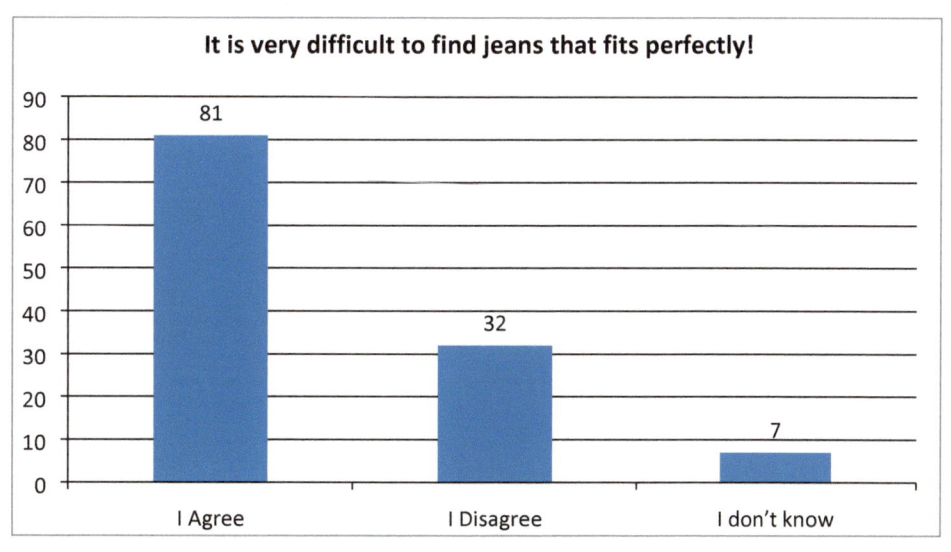

It is very difficult to find jeans that fits perfectly!

Response	Value
I Agree	81
I Disagree	32
I don't know	7

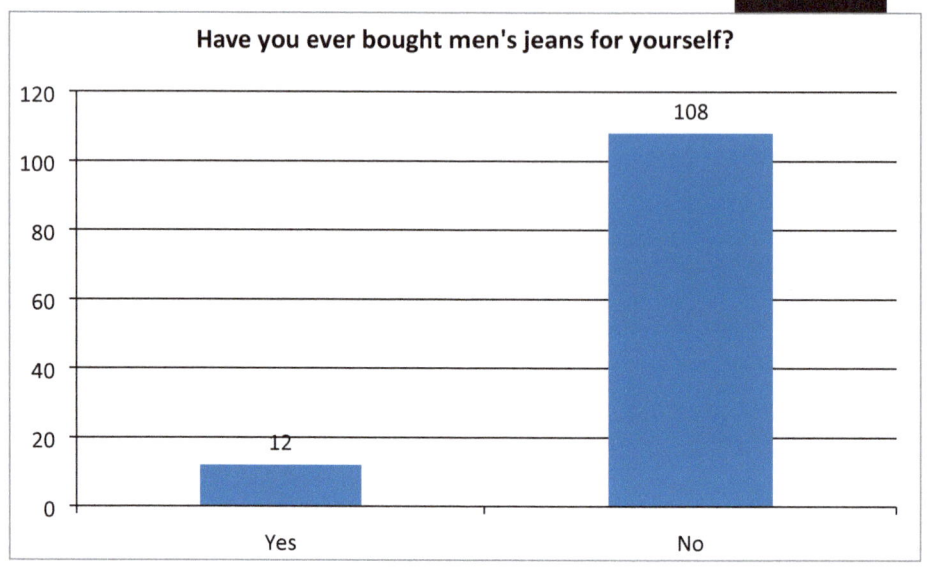

Have you ever bought men's jeans for yourself?

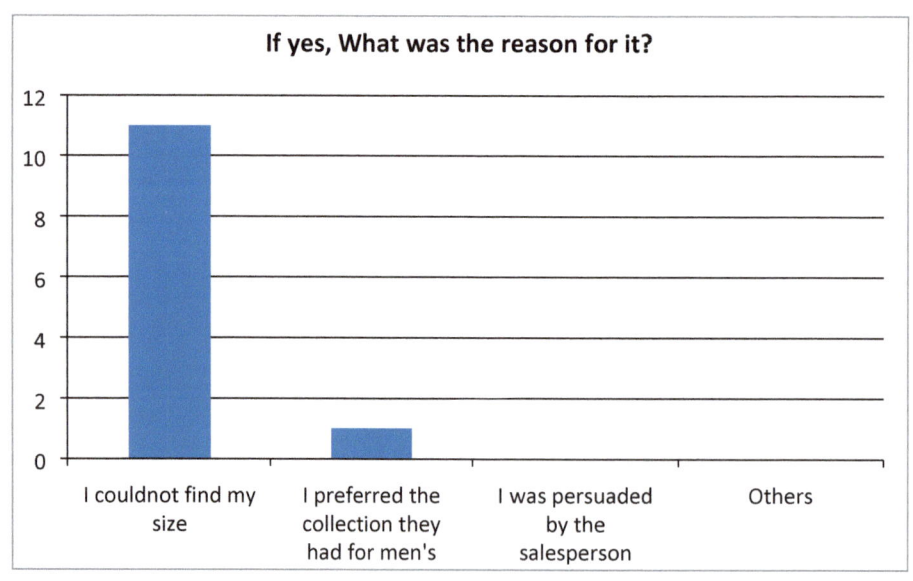

If yes, What was the reason for it?

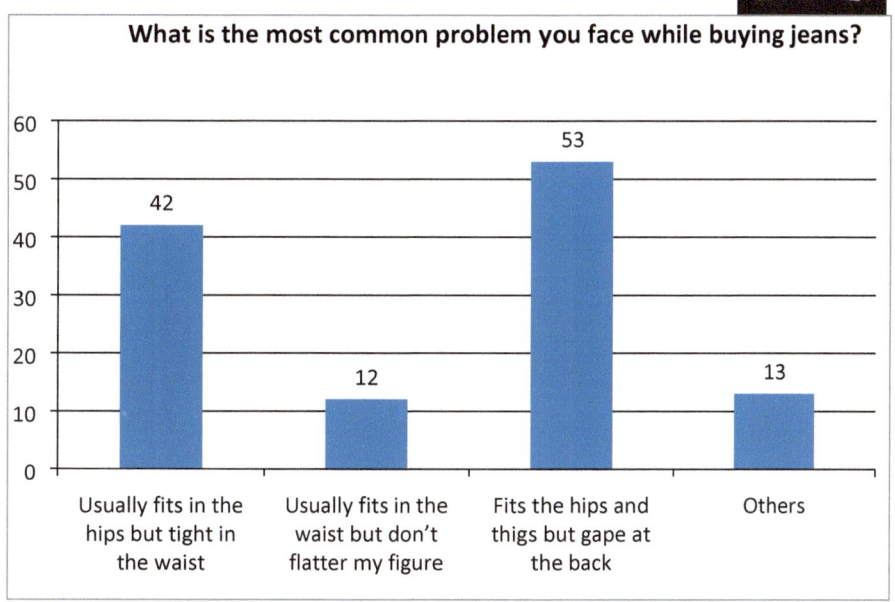

Others include – Length of the garment

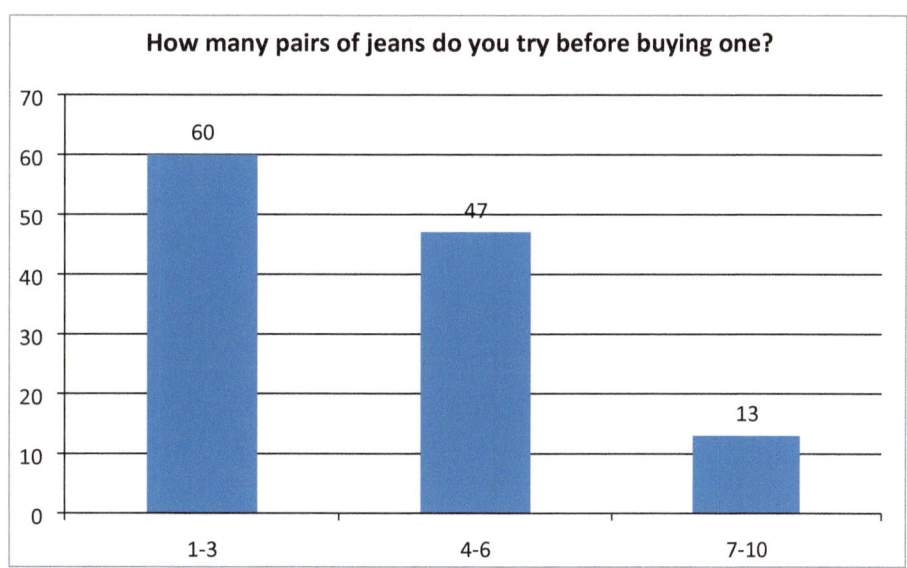

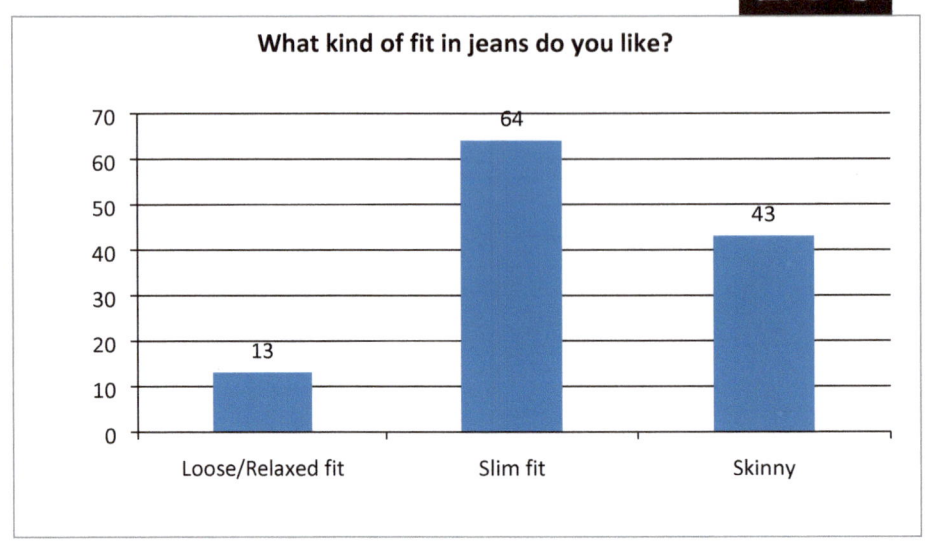

FINDINGS

During Lee store visits I found out that Lee provides women with fit problems (either bigger in size or with a different body type) , the Powell fit, which is for men.

Market Survey proves that there is a problem which women face who have a heavy bottom / flat bottom

Levi's ID Curve is the only solution available in the market for their fit problems

CONCLUSION

There is a requirement of a competitor brand in the market that can cater to the market that only Levi's has monopoly over right now. If Lee launches fits that cater to same market with better styles and more variety, we could take Levi's and also reach out to women who have a different body types.

New Fit

I have developed a fit which keeps in mind the Slight and Bold Curve and also the suggestion of the women in the survey. The Measurements are as follows:-

FIT NAME	Stacy	Jenny
Waist	30	31 1/2
Front Rise (incl. W.B)	7 1/2	7 3/4
Back Rise (incl. W.B)	12 3/4	12 1/4
Seat	37 1/4	35 1/2
Thigh	22	20 1/2
Knee	14 3/4	14 1/2
Bottom Hem	12 1/2	12